D0712096

How Do IRRIGATION SYSTEMS Work?

Charles C. Hofer

PowerKiDS press.

New York

Published in 2017 by The Rosen Publishing Group, Inc.
29 East 21st Street, New York, NY 10010

First Edition

Editor: Greg Roza
Book Design: Mickey Harmon

Photo Credits: Cover, pp. 1–32 (water) elic/Shutterstock.com; cover, pp. 1–32 (pipes) Kovalenko Alexander/Shutterstock.com; cover (image) alexmisu/Shutterstock.com; p. 5 (main) Cecilia Lim H M/Shutterstock.com; p. 5 (sprinkler) grafxart/Shutterstock.com; p. 5 (flood irrigation) https://commons.wikimedia.org/wiki/File:SiphonTubes.JPG; p. 7 loskutnikov/Shutterstock.com; p. 9 MyLoupe/Contributor/Universal Images Group/Getty Images; pp. 10, 11 trekandshoot/Shutterstock.com; p. 13 (inset) Everett Historical/Shutterstock.com; p. 15 Varts/Shutterstock.com; p. 17 (main) B Brown/Shutterstock.com; p. 17 (inset) Stefan Mokrzecki/Getty Images; p. 18 Zigzag Mountain Art/Shutterstock.com; p. 19 James L. Stanfield/Contributor/National Geographic/Getty Images; p. 21 ifong/Shutterstock.com; p. 23 Naughtynut/Shutterstock.com; p. 25 w.g.design/Shutterstock.com; p. 27 FLAVIO CONCEIÇO FOTOS/Getty Images; p. 29 goodluz/Shutterstock.com; p. 30 Zurijeta/Shutterstock.com.

Library of Congress Cataloging-in-Publication Data

Names: Hofer, Charles, author.
Title: How do irrigation systems work? / Charles C. Hofer.
Description: New York : PowerKids Press, [2016] | Series: STEM
   waterworks | Includes index.
Identifiers: LCCN 2016013445 | ISBN 9781499420074 (pbk.) | ISBN 9781499420098 (library bound) | ISBN 9781499420081 (6 pack)
Subjects: LCSH: Irrigation water–Juvenile literature. | Water-supply,
   Agricultural–Juvenile literature. | Irrigation engineering–Juvenile
   literature.
Classification: LCC S614 .H64 2016 | DDC 333.91/3–dc23
LC record available at http://lccn.loc.gov/2016013445

Manufactured in the United States of America

CPSIA Compliance Information: Batch #BS16PK: For Further Information contact Rosen Publishing, New York, New York at 1-800-237-9932

Contents

Water Is Life

Without water, there would be no life on Earth. We need water to drink. We need water to produce food. We need water to live.

The water we need is found on top of snow-capped mountains or in underground **aquifers**. It also comes from lakes and rivers and wetlands. But we need to get that water from its sources to where we can use it. Irrigation helps us capture this water and deliver it to where we need it most.

Irrigation is the application of water to land using man-made technology. It's mostly used to deliver water to farmland where it feeds thirsty crops. Humans first used irrigation techniques to transport and store water thousands of years ago. Civilizations were founded and humans flourished—thanks in large part to irrigation.

Irrigation brings water to where we need it most. Irrigation gives life to our food supply and provides us with drinking water.

In the Pipe

Water systems—which include **aqueducts**, canals, dams, **reservoirs**, sewers, and irrigation systems—are vital to the growth and prosperity of civilizations. We wouldn't have any of these important water systems without science, technology, engineering, and math. Altogether, these topics are known as STEM. Scientists and engineers need a solid understanding of these topics.

center pivot irrigation

flood irrigation

lawn sprinkler

The Water We Use

Even though Earth's surface is 71 percent water, most of it is salt water found in oceans around the world. Unfortunately, salt water is mostly useless to humans. Although technologies exist that can remove salts from salt water to make freshwater, it's too costly to be a common practice. We have to rely on our freshwater stores to maintain our food supply and to provide drinking water.

Only 2.5 percent of our planet's water is freshwater—the water we need to drink, water our crops, and provide for our animals. In the United States, more than one-third of our freshwater is used to irrigate crops and produce food. Moving this freshwater to where it's needed, such as a house or a farm, requires good irrigation practices.

Although Earth is covered in water, most of this salt water is useless for our needs. We can't drink salt water. The freshwater we do have must be managed properly to meet the demands of a growing population.

In the Pipe

Desalination is the process of removing salts from seawater to make freshwater. However, current desalination technology uses a lot of power and is extremely expensive. Only by improving these technologies can we make desalination more cost-effective to help solve water shortages.

History of Irrigation

Many ancient cultures developed methods of irrigation to help tame wild rivers and send water where it was needed. Perhaps the most successful of these cultures was that of the ancient Egyptians.

Much of Egypt is covered in vast, dry desert. Running through this land is the mighty Nile River, which provides water to this **arid** country. For centuries the Egyptians dealt with seasonal flooding that was good for crops but could also be destructive. Starting around 3000 BC, however, the Egyptians built irrigation systems that ultimately better harnessed the power of the Nile River.

In the Americas, the ancient Maya also developed irrigation systems around 1500 BC. The Maya built irrigation canals to deliver water to people living in massive cities. Irrigation helped the Maya develop into one of the greatest civilizations in the Americas.

In the Pipe

In North America, the Hohokam people of Arizona were the first people to bring water to the desert with canals that delivered water from local rivers. Their early advances in irrigation allowed the Hohokam to thrive in the harsh desert environment.

The ancient Egyptians were one of the first people to develop irrigation systems. These advances allowed the Egyptian civilization to flourish despite its arid location.

A Changing World

Our world is changing fast. The human population is growing and expanding into new areas. With all this growth, the demand for water is greater than ever before.

From wheat and rice to potatoes and pecans, plants feed our hungry world. These crops need fresh air, sunlight, soil, and, most importantly, water—lots of water! Plants need freshwater to transport **nutrients** from the soil to their root systems. This allows plants to grow big and healthy and produce the food and other products we rely on.

new housing in the desert near Las Vegas, Nevada

With a changing world sprawling into new areas, more efficient irrigation systems will be needed to deliver water to where we need it most.

Well-designed irrigation systems allow us to better use our limited water resources. Designing irrigation systems requires sound engineering and technology with a strong knowledge of earth science and math. More **efficient** forms of irrigation will be needed to meet the future demands of an increasingly crowded—and thirsty—planet.

A Good Plan

The water we use for irrigation comes in two forms: surface water and groundwater. Most of the water we use is surface water, which includes water found in rivers, lakes, and other bodies of water. The rest of the water we use is groundwater. This water must be pumped up from aquifers deep underground.

Unfortunately, groundwater aquifers can dry up through overpumping. This can also lead to severe **degradation** of soil used for crops. These problems can add up and seriously harm our food supply.

Making water supplies last requires well-planned irrigation practices. The type of irrigation usually depends on a variety of factors, such as the source of the water and what the water will be used for.

Farmers have many types of irrigation to choose from. Cost, water use, and the type of crop being produced are just a few considerations farmers must think about when selecting a form of irrigation.

In the Pipe

In the 1930s, places such as Oklahoma experienced the harmful effects of bad irrigation practices. During this time, water resources dried up and the soil became useless to farmers. Because of the "dust bowl," thousands of Oklahomans were forced to leave their homes and farms.

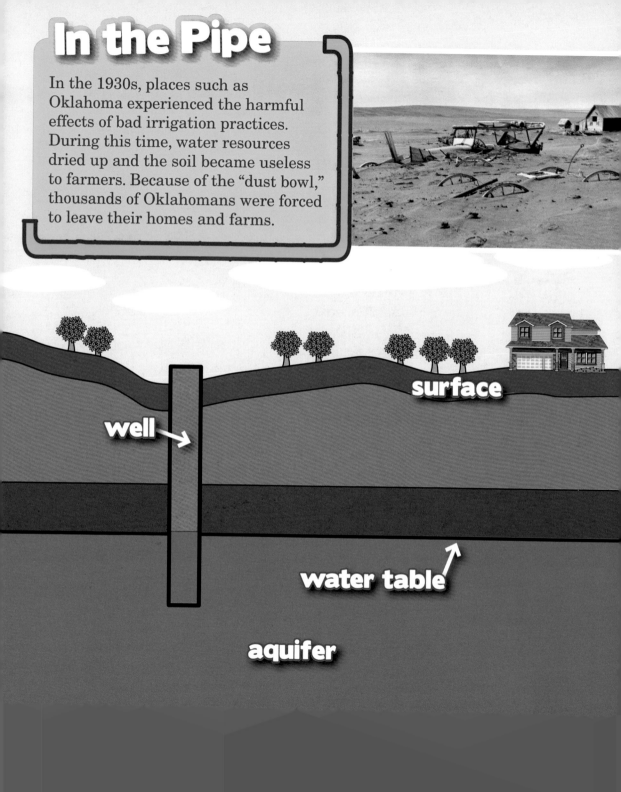

surface

well

water table

aquifer

Surface Irrigation

The most common type of irrigation used today is surface irrigation, also known as flood irrigation. The basic concepts of flood irrigation are mostly unchanged from the days of the ancient Egyptians.

With flood irrigation, water might be diverted from a river or pumped up from a groundwater aquifer. The water is then delivered to crops using canals. Furrows, or dirt ditches, hold the water and let it slowly absorb into the soil to meet the plants' roots. Gravity moves the water across the field and eventually into drainage areas.

Flood irrigation is popular because it doesn't require a lot of mechanical parts that might break down or require **maintenance**. However, flood irrigation isn't very efficient. It requires a lot of water, much of which is lost to **evaporation**.

Flood irrigation has been used since humans first started farming the land. In this image, rice seedlings grow in a paddy, or a field where rice is grown.

Overhead Irrigation

Just like the sprinkler in your backyard, overhead irrigation uses a **pressurized** system to spray water over land. Overhead irrigation is popular because it can deliver a lot of water over a large area.

Large farming operations use overhead irrigation technology such as the center pivot, water gun, or overhead boom. These are massive—and expensive—sprinkler systems that can spray water over huge fields of crops.

Overhead irrigation isn't without problems, though. A lot of water can be lost to evaporation as the water is sprayed through the air. Also, overhead irrigation covers plants with water, leaving their leaves and stems wet. This can lead to outbreaks of fungus and bacteria that can severely damage crops.

Overhead boom irrigation uses a long pipe on wheels that waters plants as it moves across a field. Center pivot irrigation also uses a long pipe, but one end stays in place while the other swings in a wide circle.

center pivot irrigation

overhead boom irrigation

Drip Irrigation

Drip irrigation is a very efficient water delivery system. It is used mostly in smaller **horticulture** operations to grow produce, such as tomatoes and peppers. For this type of irrigation, crops are planted in rows. A **complex** series of hoses delivers water to individual plants. Connected to the tubes are emitters, which are small spouts that let water slowly trickle out.

Drip irrigation is popular because it's a very precise form of irrigation, unlike flood irrigation. Thanks to the hoses and emitters, producers can target specific plants instead of entire fields of crops. However, drip irrigation can be very costly. It requires a lot of planning and constant maintenance to fix tubes and unclog emitters.

emitter

Drip irrigation is often used in greenhouses because it can deliver water to specific plants in a controlled environment.

Subsurface Irrigation

Subsurface irrigation works much like drip irrigation by using a system of hoses and emitters. However, this type of irrigation occurs underground where plants need water most. Whether in a greenhouse or in an agricultural field, producers must first dig long trenches to bury irrigation lines. If there's a break in a line or an emitter clogs up, the line must be dug up and fixed. Repairs can be costly and time-consuming.

However, subsurface irrigation has many benefits. First, there's little water lost to evaporation. Over time, this can save a lot of water—and money—for the producer. Secondly, water can be delivered directly to the plant's roots. This allows the plant to grow faster and heartier than if the water was delivered on the soil's surface.

Subsurface irrigation delivers water directly to the plant's root zone where it can be used more efficiently.

emitters

The Water Cycle

There's only a certain amount of water for people, plants, and animals to use. Understanding how this water moves around our planet is important when **conserving** our water resources.

The water cycle explains how all the water on Earth changes from one form to another and moves from place to place. Ice, rain, fog, a rushing river, and a mucky pond are all parts of the water cycle. This water travels around Earth through processes such as evaporation, **precipitation**, **transpiration**, and others.

Just as irrigation is the artificial movement of water from place to place, the water cycle is the natural movement of this same water. Using science to better understand the water cycle can help us build more efficient irrigation systems to meet our growing demand for water.

Understanding how water moves through the water cycle can help us better conserve our water resources.

precipitation

condensation

runoff

evaporation

transpiration

In the Pipe

Freshwater still contains small amounts of salts. When water evaporates, these salts are left behind. They build up and can be harmful to plants and soil. Proper irrigation helps drain soil and prevents salt buildup.

Technology to the Rescue

New irrigation technology can help conserve our water supply. Today, many of these new methods are used to irrigate gardens, lawns, and parks to help reduce water use.

When it rains, most rainwater washes down the drain. Rainwater harvesting uses irrigation technology to capture and store the water that falls from the sky. This rainwater can then be used to irrigate gardens or other locations. Rainwater harvesting helps cut down on water use—and it saves homeowners money on their water bill, too!

In the Pipe

Many cities are increasing their use of reclaimed water, which is recycled sewer water that has been treated to remove waste and other harmful things. Reclaimed water can be used to irrigate crops or returned to lakes and rivers to benefit wildlife.

Golf courses require a lot of water to keep them green for golfers. Many courses have started using gray water and reclaimed water to keep their grass green and healthy and save money at the same time.

Gray water is another way to help conserve our water supply. Gray water is recycled water from sinks, showers, washing machines, and other places in our homes and businesses. Creative systems collect gray water that can then be used again around the home, such as for toilet flushing or to irrigate home gardens.

Adding It Up

Food producers need to **maximize** their yield (crops produced) while reducing use of profit-eating resources such as labor, fertilizer, or water. Using mathematical equations helps producers save money on their farming operations.

Water budgets describe how much water will be needed to properly water a certain area. Managers develop water budgets by using things like infiltration rate (the rate water is absorbed into soil) or evaporation rate (the rate water is lost to evaporation). An area's annual rainfall or the type of crops being planted will also be used to develop a water budget.

Using too little or too much water can harm crops and ruin an entire season of work! These mathematical equations help maximize water irrigation efficiency. Math allows producers to get a greater yield from less water.

Using water budget equations like this one helps producers get the most out of their crops with the lowest cost.

precipitation + groundwater

— evaporation + transpiration + runoff

---

change in water storage

Science at Work

Many fields of science must come together to make irrigation work better. For example, hydrology is the study of water. A hydrologist studies how water moves through our environment or what factors influence water quality and quantity.

Soil science plays an important role in irrigation too. Soil scientists study soil chemistry and soil type to understand how water, nutrients, and plants interact. Soil science is not only important for raising crops but also for waste management, forest management, and even the management of golf courses.

Ecosystems scientists specialize in how natural systems work. Like the water cycle, the nitrogen cycle and carbon cycle move precious materials from place to place. These elements play important roles in growing our food or cleaning our air and water.

Scientists from different fields must work together to help conserve our water supply for future generations.

Water for Tomorrow

Nobody knows what the future holds, but we can be certain that many challenges lie ahead of us. The human population is growing rapidly and we will need to produce more food with less land and less water. Our climate is changing too. Many areas are becoming hotter and drier and putting more stress on food producers around the world.

The next generation of scientists, engineers, and mathematicians will have to work together to meet the needs of our changing world. Better designed, more efficient irrigation systems must be developed in order to meet growing demand for our precious water. Our lives depend on it.

Glossary

aqueduct: A pathway constructed to guide water from a source into a populated area.

aquifer: A layer of rock or sand that absorbs and holds water.

arid: Having little or no rain.

complex: Having to do with something with many parts that work together.

conserve: To keep something from harm and not waste it.

degradation: The act or process of ruining something.

efficient: Capable of producing desired results without wasting materials, time, or energy.

evaporation: The process of water changing into water vapor.

horticulture: The science of growing fruits, vegetables, flowers, or ornamental plants.

maintenance: The act of taking care of something, or maintaining it.

maximize: To increase something as much as possible.

nutrient: Something a living thing needs to grow and stay alive.

precipitation: Rain, snow, sleet, or hail.

pressurized: Built to maintain an interior pressure greater than the air outside.

reservoir: A man-made lake used for storing water.

transpiration: The process by which plants give off water vapor through openings in their leaves.

Index

Websites

Due to the changing nature of Internet links, PowerKids Press has developed an online list of websites related to the subject of this book. This site is updated regularly. Please use this link to access the list: www.powerkidslinks.com/sww/irri